My Middle School Crush

The Avery Diary Book 3

By
Lucky Fish Press
Copyright ©2025

CONTENTS

Chapter One   3

Chapter Two   6

Chapter Three   10

Chapter Four   14

Chapter Five   17

Chapter Six   21

Chapter Seven   26

Chapter Eight   30

Chapter Nine   34

Chapter Ten   37

Chapter Eleven   40

Chapter Twelve   44

1. He Sat Next to ME

Big news: I'm going to marry Jason... you know, eventually. Sure, he doesn't know it yet, and yeah, he barely remembers my name half the time, but that's just a minor detail. True love takes time. Right now, I'm focusing on phase one: *Operation: Get Him to Notice Me Without Falling Over.* Spoiler alert: it's not going great.

Today starts with what I call "Locker Chaos 3000." Picture this: I'm trying to open my locker, but of course, it's jammed shut. I'm yanking on the handle like I'm in some kind of strongman competition when Jason—THE Jason—walks by. My heart stops. My hands get sweaty. And that's when the locker decides to unjam itself, launching me backward into the garbage can.

"Uh... are you okay, Amy?" Jason asks, pulling me up by my backpack strap like I'm a stray kitten.
"IT'S AVERY!" I blurt out way louder than necessary. My voice echoes down the hallway. Everyone stares. Great start to the day.

Jason scratches his head, looking a little embarrassed. "Oh, right. Sorry, Avery." Then he smiles. Not just any smile—the kind of smile that could melt steel beams. I'm about to say something cute and clever when the bell rings, and he walks off, leaving me standing there like a trash-themed statue.

WHY IS THIS MY LIFE?!!!

At lunch, I'm still recovering from the locker incident when the unthinkable happens: Jason sits down *at MY TABLE.* Not just near me. Not just in the general cafeteria area. Right. Across. From. Me.

My Bestie Claire's face looks like she's just discovered soda. My other Bestie Ellie starts whispering furiously, and I catch words like "jackpot" and "betting pool." Turns out, they're taking bets on how fast I'll embarrass myself in front of Jason.

"Two minutes," Claire says, shoving a crumpled five dollar bill into Ellie's hand.
"Thirty seconds," Ellie counters, grinning like a crazy person.

I'm about to prove them wrong when Jason looks right at me. "Hey, Avery, what's up?" he says, like we're old friends or something.

"Uh, nothing much," I reply, trying to act casual. Then, because my brain has officially left the building, I add, "Just sitting here, eating food... *with my mouth.*"

Claire snorts so hard she almost chokes on her juice box. Ellie looks like she's won the lottery. Jason, bless his perfect heart, just nods like I'm making sense.

After lunch, I decide to hide out in the library until the humiliation fog clears. But, of course, that's where Carl, my *annoying little brother*, decides to show up. Apparently, his class is having "library time," which really just means "find ways to annoy your sister" time.

"Hey, Avery!" Carl shouts across the room, waving a paper above his head. "Guess what I drew today?"

Before I can stop him, he runs over and slaps it onto the table in front of me. It's a picture of me and Jason... in wedding clothes. "Introducing Mr. and Mrs. Avery Carter!" he announces loudly, like he's at a freakin' awards show.

"Carl, go away," I hiss, trying to stuff the drawing into my backpack. But it's too late. Jason walks in, holding a library book, and sees the whole thing.

"What's that?" Jason asks, leaning over the table.

"Oh, uh, nothing!" I stammer, shoving the paper under my notebook.

Carl, the little demon, grins. "It's her future wedding photo." Then he points at Jason and adds, "She thinks you're cute."

Jason's face goes red, and mine feels like it's literally on fire. "Uh, cool," he says, backing away like the table's about to explode.

"Carl, I'm going to end you," I mutter as Jason escapes to the other side of the library.

By the time I get home, I'm ready to crawl into a hole and live there forever. But Grandpa has other plans. "You look like you've seen a ghost," he says, plopping down next to me on the couch.

"More like I *became* the ghost," I reply, burying my face in a pillow.

"Boy troubles?" Grandpa asks, wiggling his eyebrows. I groan. WHY DOES EVERYONE IN THIS FAMILY HAVE TO BE SO NOSY?

Grandpa, of course, takes my groan as an invitation to give me "life advice." He starts talking about how he met Grandma by spilling hot soup on her shoes??? and somehow, that led to true love. "The key," he says, "is confidence. You've gotta act like you're the prize."

"Grandpa, I tripped into a garbage can this morning," I remind him. "I am NO prize."

"You're my prize, Aves" Grandpa says with a smile, which is sweet, but also doesn't help me AT ALL.

Later, as I'm writing this, I hear Carl outside my door. He's humming the wedding march. I'm seriously considering throwing a shoe at him.

Tomorrow, I'm going to avoid Jason AT ALL COSTS. Probably. Unless he sits next to me at lunch again. In that case, I'll just... try not to talk about eating with my mouth. Baby steps, Avery. Baby steps.

2. The Jason Fan Club

BIG NEWS: Jason needs my help. With English homework. That's right— *my* English help. He says it's because I give off a "smart girl vibe," which is code for "I'm failing, and you were the only person left in the hallway when I thought of this."

Does it matter? No. Because in the romance movie playing in my head, this is the part where we lock eyes over a study guide, and he says, "Wow, Avery, you're so smart and cool and not at all awkward." Then we fall in love, and he forgets all about popular girl Taylor and her perfect hair.

Anyway, here's how it starts: I'm standing by my locker, trying to jam my social studies book into my bag, when Jason strolls up like he doesn't have a care in the world.

"Hey, Avery," he says, leaning casually against the locker next to mine. "I need a favor."

For a second, I think maybe he's going to ask me to prom (yes, I know we're only in middle school, but a girl can dream). Instead, he says, "Can you help me with my English homework? I'm kinda lost."

My brain short-circuits. Jason. Needs. My. Help.

"SURE!" I say, probably a little too loud and too enthusiastically.

Behind him, Claire and Ellie pop up like groundhogs. They're both whispering to each other. I hear phrases like "future couple alert" and "IT'S FINALLY HAPPENING."

Later, during lunch, Claire and Ellie won't shut up about how this is my "big break." Ellie even pulls out a napkin and starts drawing a heart with "Avery + Jason = HEART" in the middle. I snatch it out of her hands and throw it in the trash, but my face is basically a tomato. A Pomegranate. A watermelon inside out. I can't think of anymore red fruits.

"You better not mess this up," Claire says, wagging a carrot stick at me.

"No pressure," Ellie adds with a grin.

No pressure? Are they kidding? This is Jason we're talking about. My middle school crush. My future husband. And now he's coming over to my house for tutoring. I spend the rest of the day trying not to freak out.

When I get home, I'm ready to turn our living room into the ultimate study zone. I hide all the embarrassing stuff: Carl's action figures, Grandpa's crossword puzzles, the framed picture of me dressed as a cabbage in kindergarten. Everything is perfect.

Then Carl gets home.

"What's going on?" he asks, immediately suspicious.

"Nothing," I say, a little too quickly.

Carl squints at me. "You're acting weird. Is someone coming over?"

Before I can lie, the doorbell rings. It's Jason. Of course, Carl sprints to the door before I can stop him.

"What's that?" Jason asks, pointing at the giant cardboard sign taped to our front door. It says, "WELCOME TO THE JASON FAN CLUB!!!" in Carl's absolutely terrible handwriting.

I shove Carl out of the way and rip the sign down. "Ignore that," I say, pretending I'm not dying of embarrassment.

Jason just laughs. "Cool. I've never had a fan club before."

We sit at the kitchen table, and I pull out my English textbook. Jason pulls out a notebook with exactly one word written on it: *Help.*

"Okay," I say, trying to sound professional. "What are you stuck on?"

Jason flips to a page covered in doodles. "It's this metaphor thing. I don't get it."

"Metaphors are easy," I say. "They're comparisons. Like, 'Life is a roller coaster.'"

Jason frowns. "Why would life be a roller coaster? That doesn't make sense."

"It's not literal," I explain. "It's just a way to say life has ups and downs."

Jason looks even more confused. "So... it's not about an actual roller coaster?"

"No," I say.

Jason leans back in his chair, crossing his arms. "This is why English is so hard. If it's not about a roller coaster, why say it is?"

At this point, Carl pops up out of nowhere, holding a slice of pizza. "What's a metaphor?" he asks, his mouth full.

I sigh. "It's a figure of speech. Like, comparing one thing to another."

Carl looks at Jason. "So it's like pizza?"

Jason perks up. "Yeah! Like, life is a pizza."

"No," I groan. "It's not always about pizza."

Grandpa walks in, holding his crossword puzzle. "What's this about pizza?"

For the next ten minutes, I try to explain metaphors to Jason, Carl, and Grandpa. It's like talking to a wall. A very loud, very pizza-obsessed wall.

"Life is a pizza," Carl says, holding up his slice. "You've got the cheese, which is the good stuff, and the crust, which is boring but necessary."

"And the pepperoni is the exciting parts!" Jason adds, looking proud of himself.

"Exactly," Grandpa says, nodding. "See, Avery? We're geniuses."

I put my head on the table. This is my life now.

After an hour of chaos, Jason finally writes down a metaphor that actually makes sense: "Homework is a monster that eats my free time and my soul."

"That's perfect," I say, relieved.

Jason grins. "See? I knew I could do it."

When he leaves, Carl shouts, "Bye, Jason! Don't forget about your fan club!" I slam the door in Carl's face, but Jason just laughs.

Dear Diary,

Lesson of the day: Metaphors are NOT like pizza. But Jason thinks they are, and somehow, that's kind of... cute? Maybe Claire and Ellie are right. Maybe this *is* my big break.

Or maybe I'm just the president of the Jason Fan Club.

3. Jealousy, Glitter, and Disaster

Dear Diary,

Today, something magical (and also horrifying) happens at school. A new girl arrives. Her name is Taylor, and she doesn't *walk* into the building—she *floats*.

I swear, she's surrounded by an invisible cloud of glitter, unicorn dust, and probably the scent of a very expensive European perfume. She's wearing this jacket that looks like it came straight out of a Paris fashion show, sparkly boots that scream "I'm too cool for this cafeteria," and her hair? It's shiny. Like, unnaturally shiny. I'm pretty sure birds would build nests in it if they could.

"Who's that?" Claire whispers as we all watch Taylor glide down the hallway like she's on a red carpet.

Ellie leans over and stage-whispers, "I heard she spent a semester in Europe. She probably speaks, like, seven languages and drinks cappuccinos for breakfast."

I roll my eyes. "Big deal. I've been to Canada. Twice."

Then Taylor does something unexpected. She walks *right up to me.*

"Hi!" Taylor says, flashing a smile so bright it could power the school's Wi-Fi. "I love your socks. Mismatched is so *in* right now."

I blink at her. Did she just... compliment me?

For the record, my socks are not a fashion statement. I couldn't find a matching pair this morning because Carl was using one of my favorite socks to dress up his action figures. (Don't ask.)

"Uh, thanks," I mumble, suddenly feeling very self-conscious about my ketchup stain from lunch.

"No problem," Taylor says, giving me another dazzling smile before she twirls away like she's auditioning for a shampoo commercial.

As soon as she's out of earshot, Claire and Ellie pounce.

"Did you hear that? She talked to you!" Claire hisses.
"She likes your socks! You're basically best friends now!" Ellie adds, practically bouncing with excitement.

"Calm down," I say, trying to play it cool. But inside, my brain is screaming: *Taylor thinks I'm cool!*

Things take a turn for the worse at lunch.

Jason walks into the cafeteria, carrying his tray like he's auditioning for a toothpaste commercial. Seriously, how does someone's hair always look like it's styled by a wind machine? It's unnatural.

I'm about to wave him over to sit with us when I notice something unexpected—and a little unsettling. Jason is waving.

Not at me. At Taylor.

Taylor waves back, her sparkly bracelets jingling like tiny bells. Then, to my absolute shock, she pats the seat next to her, and Jason actually sits down.

"What's going on here?" I mutter to Claire and Ellie, trying not to stare too hard in their direction.

"Maybe he's asking her about Europe," Ellie says, her tone annoyingly reasonable.

"Yeah, maybe," Claire adds. "Or maybe she's showing him how to sparkle in a cafeteria. Look at her—she makes eating a sandwich look like an art form."

It's true. Somehow, Taylor manages to eat her lunch while looking effortlessly cool. Meanwhile, I have spaghetti sauce on my chin and a cracker crumb in my hair.

"She's just… shiny," I say, poking at my mashed potatoes. "And perfect. It's annoying."

Ellie shrugs. "Shiny doesn't mean better."

"Yeah," Claire says. "And don't forget: *you* have mismatched socks. That's a statement."

I groan. Somehow, that doesn't make me feel better.

After lunch, I try to avoid thinking about Taylor. It doesn't work. She's everywhere. In the hallway, she's surrounded by a group of kids who are hanging onto her every word. In class, she answers a question about World War II and manages to make it sound like a TED Talk. Even the teachers seem impressed.

By the end of the day, I'm exhausted. Taylor is like a walking, talking reminder that I am Not Cool™.

On the way home, Claire and Ellie try to cheer me up.

"You've got something she doesn't," Ellie says.

"Yeah?" I ask, perking up.

"Historical knowledge about sock puppets," Claire says with a grin.

I groan. "Thanks, guys. That's super helpful."

When I get home, I find Carl in the living room, using Grandpa as a test subject for his latest "science experiment." Grandpa has spaghetti noodles taped to his head and looks like he's regretting all his life choices.

"What's going on here?" I ask, dropping my backpack by the door.

"I'm turning Grandpa into an alien," Carl says proudly.

"Obviously," Grandpa mutters.

Normally, I'd laugh, but today I'm too busy sulking. I flop onto the couch and let out a dramatic sigh.

"What's wrong with you?" Carl asks, tilting his head.

"Nothing," I snap.

"Boy troubles," Grandpa says wisely. "It's always boy troubles."

"It's not boy troubles!" I yell, even though, okay, it kind of is.

"Is this about that Jason kid?" Carl asks, grinning like he knows all my secrets. "Because if it is, you're doomed. I saw him talking to that new girl. What's her name? Sparkles?"

"Taylor," I correct him, groaning.

"She seems nice," Carl says. "Nice hair. Very shiny."

"That's not helpful, Carl," I mutter.

Later, while I'm doing my homework, I can't stop replaying lunch in my head. Jason sitting next to Taylor. Taylor waving her sparkly bracelets around like she's royalty. Everyone looking at her like she's the best thing since sliced bread.

I glance down at my mismatched socks and sigh.

Maybe I'm overthinking this. Maybe Taylor isn't trying to steal Jason. Maybe she's just being nice. And maybe I'm just jealous because she seems so perfect and confident.

Or maybe, as Claire would say, it's all part of her master plan.

Either way, one thing is clear: Taylor isn't going anywhere. And if I want to win Jason's heart, I need a plan.

Tomorrow, the gloves are coming off. (Figuratively, of course. I don't actually own gloves.)

Dear Diary,

Lesson of the day: Sometimes, the sparkly new girl isn't the enemy. But she is super annoying. Stay tuned.

4. Jake, Jason, and Mashed Potato Chaos

Dear Diary,

Today is one of those days where the universe decides to mess with me for fun. It starts when my locker refuses to open. AGAIN.

For some reason, my locker thinks it's an escape room, and I've failed every challenge. I'm pulling, yanking, even kicking it when suddenly, I hear someone behind me say, "Need help, Captain Clumsy?"

It's Jake. Jake, my *ex*-best friend, who used to call me Captain Clumsy every time I tripped over something—which, for the record, was a lot.

I groan. "Go away, Jake. I've got this."

"You sure about that?" he says, smirking like he's the locker whisperer.

"Positive," I snap, giving the locker one last mighty yank. Spoiler: it doesn't open. Instead, I nearly dislocate my shoulder.

Jake sighs like he's dealing with a toddler. "Step aside."

Before I can protest, he gives my locker one swift bang on the side, and— *click*—it opens. Just like that.

"Seriously?" I glare at him.

He grins. "What can I say? Lockers love me."

Fast forward to lunch. I'm balancing my tray like it's the Olympic event for clumsiness when disaster strikes.

One wrong step, and my tray wobbles. Then, in slow motion, I watch my mashed potatoes launch into the air like a creamy, starchy missile.

Guess where they land?

Jason's head.

Yes, Jason. The guy whose hair looks like it's sponsored by a shampoo company. Now it's a mashed potato masterpiece.

There's a collective gasp in the cafeteria. Jason freezes, his perfectly gelled hair oozing potatoes.

"Oh no," Ellie whispers.

"Oh yes," Claire whispers back, clearly enjoying this.

I want to disappear into the floor, but instead, I mumble, "Uh... sorry?"

Before Jason can respond, someone starts laughing. Loudly.

It's Jake.

"Nice shot, Captain Clumsy," he says, grinning at me like this is the funniest thing he's ever seen.

I glare at him. "Not. Helping."

But then he says, "Don't worry. It's just a food attack. Happens to the best of us."

And for some reason, that makes me laugh.

Later, I'm sitting outside on the steps, trying to recover from the Great Potato Incident of Lunch. That's when Jake shows up again, because apparently, he's everywhere today.

"Hey," he says, sitting down next to me like it's no big deal.

"Hey," I mumble, still mortified.

He nudges me. "Look, if it makes you feel better, Jason needed a new hairstyle. Potato chic is very in right now."

I snort. "Yeah, I'm sure he'll thank me later."

Jake grins. "Exactly. You're doing him a favor."

For a moment, it's like old times. Jake and I used to sit on these same steps, joking about everything and nothing. Back before middle school and "Puberty" turned him into someone I didn't recognize. *Someone cooler.*

Wait. Cooler?

I shake my head. No, no, no. Jake is *not* cooler. He's Jake. The kid who used to burp the alphabet and eat pizza rolls with ketchup.

But then he says, "You know, you're still the same Avery. You just overthink everything now."

I blink at him. "What's that supposed to mean?"

He shrugs. "I don't know. Maybe you should stop worrying so much and just... be yourself."

"Easy for you to say," I mutter.

Jake laughs. "Yeah, because I'm perfect."

I roll my eyes, but secretly, his words stick with me.

Dear Diary,

Lesson of the day: Sometimes, the universe sends mashed potatoes flying to remind you of things you didn't realize you missed. Like Jake. And maybe, just maybe, I don't hate him as much as I thought.

To be continued...

5. Puppets, Granola, and Locker Graffiti

Dear Diary,

Let me just say this: tutoring Jason is like explaining algebra to Carl, my little brother. Except Carl actually listens sometimes.

We're sitting at one of those squeaky library tables, surrounded by stacks of books that Jason hasn't touched, and I'm trying—*trying*—to help him understand *Romeo and Juliet*.

"So, it's about love," I say, pointing to the book. "And tragedy. Like, their families hate each other, but they fall in love anyway."

Jason looks at me blankly. "Sounds like a zombie apocalypse."

I blink. "What?"

"Yeah," he says, leaning back in his chair like he's cracked the code of life. "Two people in a town overrun by zombies. Their families are zombie clans, and they fall in love but, like, can't be together because they'll get bitten."

I stare at him. "Jason, *Romeo and Juliet* is not about zombies."

"It could be," he says, nodding like he's a genius.

This is when I realize I need a Plan B. And by Plan B, I mean sock puppets.

Ten minutes later, I have a Juliet sock on my left hand and a Romeo sock on my right. Juliet has yarn hair. Romeo has a Sharpie mustache.

"Okay, Jason," I say, holding up the puppets. "Let's try this again."

I make Romeo say, "Oh, Juliet, I love you!" Then I make Juliet say, "But Romeo, our families hate each other!"

Jason watches this like he's at a sports game. "So, when do the zombies show up?"

I sigh. "There are. No. Zombies."

Just then, Taylor floats by. And I mean *floats*—her skirt swishes, her hair glows, and she smells like vanilla cupcakes.

She claps politely. "Sock puppets? That's so creative, Avery."

"Uh, thanks?" I say, feeling my face turn red.

Taylor pulls a little box out of her tote bag and sets it on the table. "Here. Handmade granola bars. They're shaped like hearts!"

Jason lights up. "Cool! Thanks, Taylor!"

I watch as Jason grabs a granola bar and takes a huge bite. Meanwhile, Taylor smiles at me like she's a fairy godmother.

"You're doing a great job, Avery," she says sweetly before walking off.

I can't explain it, but for some reason, her compliment makes me feel… weird. And not the good kind of weird.

After our *totally successful* tutoring session (read: total disaster), I head to my locker, hoping for some peace.

Big mistake.

Scrawled across my locker in PERMANENT MARKER are the words:

"Avery + Jason = True Love"

My brain short-circuits.

"WHO DID THIS?" I yell, waving my arms like a maniac.

Claire and Ellie appear out of nowhere, staring at the graffiti.

"Oh wow," Ellie says. "That's bold."

Claire grins. "I give it a solid 9/10 for effort. But they could've added glitter."

"This is not funny!" I hiss. "Do you know how hard it is to get permanent marker off metal?"

Ellie shrugs. "Maybe it's fate."

"Fate needs to learn how to use a whiteboard." I snap.

I do what any mature person would do: I hide in the library.

I'm sitting behind a giant stack of books when Jake shows up. How does he always know where to find me?

"Nice locker art," he says, sitting down in the chair across from me.

I groan. "Don't start."

He grins. "Relax. I'm here to help."

"With what? Making it worse?"

"Nope," Jake says, holding up a roll of duct tape. "I brought supplies."

I stare at him. "What are you planning to do? Tape over it?"

"Exactly," he says, pulling out a second item: a tiny jar of glitter.

"Duct tape and glitter?" I say, raising an eyebrow.

He nods. "It's foolproof. Trust me."

Fifteen minutes later, we're standing in front of my locker. Jake carefully covers the marker with a strip of duct tape, then sprinkles glitter on top.

"There," he says proudly. "Problem solved."

I fold my arms. "Yeah, except now my locker looks like it belongs to a unicorn."

Jake shrugs. "Better than people thinking you're writing love notes to yourself."

I gasp. "Wait—you think people will think *I* wrote that?"

Jake smirks. "Well, it *is* your locker…"

"Great," I mutter. "Now I'm the girl who's in love with her own locker."

But then Jake laughs, and somehow, it's hard to stay mad.

Dear Diary,

Today's lesson: Sock puppets can't teach Shakespeare, duct tape can fix everything, and Jake is annoyingly good at making me laugh when I don't want to.

Also, if I find out who wrote on my locker, they're getting a face full of glitter.

6.Winking and Makeover Madness

Dear Diary,

Let me tell you something: when Grandpa decides to give you dating advice, **run.**

It all starts at breakfast. Grandpa is slurping his black coffee—it's so strong I'm pretty sure it could power a small rocket—and reading his *Old People Weekly* or something. I'm busy inhaling peanut butter toast because I overslept (again), when Grandpa suddenly slams his magazine down with a dramatic *thud*.

"Avery," he says, pointing at me like I've committed a crime, "you need a romantic edge."

I pause mid-chew. "A what?"

"You know! Allure! Boys like mystery! And charm!"

I stare at him. "Grandpa, the last boy I talked to was Carl's friend Pete, and he only said, 'Move, nerd.'"

Grandpa waves his hand dismissively. "That's because you're missing the basics. But don't worry, I'm here to help."

Oh no.

Lesson One: The Art of the Wink

Later that day, and Grandpa has set up "Romance Boot Camp" in the living room. He's made a sign that says **"Grandpa's Guide to Flirting for Dummies"** and taped it to the TV.

"Lesson one: The Wink," he announces, doing a demo. His wink is so over-the-top that I can't tell if he's flirting or having a stroke.

"Your turn," he says, motioning to me.

I try to wink, but my whole face scrunches up like I've bitten into a lemon.

Grandpa groans. "No, no, no! You're winking with your *soul,* not your eye. Be subtle! Be smooth!"

I try again. This time, I look like I'm staring directly into the sun.

Grandpa shakes his head. "This is hopeless. You look like a confused pirate. Just practice on someone!"

Disaster Wink Practice

At school, I decide to practice on someone random. I spot a kid from my math class near the lockers and think, *Okay, this is it. Time to nail the wink.*

What happens next cannot be described as "nailing" anything.

I wink, but it's more of a full-body convulsion. My shoulder twitches, my neck jerks, and I'm pretty sure my face temporarily folds in half.

The kid stares at me in horror. "Uh... do you need, like, medical help?"

"NOPE!" I squeak, speed-walking away like my life depends on it.

By the time I get to the bathroom, my face is bright red, and my eye won't stop twitching. Grandpa's advice is officially canceled.

Claire and Ellie's Plan of Chaos

During lunch, Claire and Ellie decide I need more help than Grandpa can provide.

"You need a makeover," Claire declares, stabbing her spaghetti like she's planning world domination.

"Yeah," Ellie chimes in. "Like, a *wow* makeover."

"No way," I say. "I'm fine the way I am."

Claire raises an eyebrow. "Avery, you're wearing socks with flamingos on them."

"So? Flamingos are cool!"

Ellie shakes her head. "We're not saying you're uncool. We're saying... you could be cooler."

"Like a shiny penny instead of a rusty nickel," Claire adds.

"That's not even a compliment," I mutter, but they're already plotting.

The Makeover of Doom

After school, I find myself in Ellie's room, which is now a full-blown "makeover station." There are hairbrushes, makeup palettes, and about 17 cans of hairspray scattered around.

Claire grabs a curling iron and starts attacking my hair like she's taming a wild lion. Ellie sprays so much hairspray that I'm pretty sure the hole in the ozone layer just got bigger.

By the time they're done, my hair looks like a cross between a bird's nest and a cotton candy machine explosion.

"Perfect!" Claire says, stepping back to admire her work.

I look in the mirror and scream internally.

Next, they move on to makeup. Ellie smears bright blue eyeshadow on my eyelids while Claire applies lipstick that's so red it could stop traffic.

"This color is called 'Crimson Kiss,'" Claire says proudly.

"It's called 'Clown Attack,'" I mutter.

Finally, they make me try on a frilly pink dress that looks like it escaped from a haunted Victorian doll collection.

"Absolutely not," I say.

"Come on, it's vintage!" Ellie pleads.

"It belongs to a ghost!" I reply, but they force me into it anyway.

Carl's Commentary

When I go back home, Carl is waiting at the door. He takes one look at me and bursts out laughing.

"What happened to you? Did you lose a bet?"

"Shut up, Carl!" I snap, trying to chase him down the hall.

Unfortunately, the dress is so long that I trip over it and nearly faceplant. Carl is still laughing as he runs into his room and slams the door.

"Not a word of this to anyone!" I yell after him.

The Next Day: Epic Disaster

The next day, Claire and Ellie insist I go to school in the "new me" outfit.

Jason notices me immediately. "Hey, uh… nice dress."

"Thanks!" I say, trying to sound confident.

Then I turn too quickly, and the dress gets caught on a chair. The sound of fabric ripping echoes through the hallway.

Claire and Ellie rush to cover me with their backpacks while Jason looks away awkwardly.

"Okay," I whisper to myself, "this cannot get worse."

It gets worse.

During English class, I decide to try Grandpa's second piece of advice: "Be mysterious."

When Jason asks me, "What's the homework again?" I reply, "Homework is just a social construct."

Jason blinks. "Uh... okay?"

Claire and Ellie overhear and burst into laughter so loud that Mr. Jenkins gives us all detention.

Lesson Learned

Dear Diary,

Today I learned:

1. *Grandpa should never give advice.*
2. *Claire and Ellie are chaos in human form.*
3. *Flamingo socks are underrated.*

Also, winking is banned. FOREVER.

7. Socks, Quizzes, and Confusion

It's weird how I always thought I was the queen of "knowing exactly what's going on." But right now, I have absolutely no idea what is happening with my life.

Take lunch today, for example. I was sitting there, minding my own business (and by "minding my own business," I mean picking at my mashed potatoes because they looked suspiciously like foam packing peanuts), when I look up and see Jason and Taylor talking across the cafeteria. Not only were they talking, but they were laughing. Together. Laughing at one of Jason's weird metaphors. Seriously, who laughs at *zombie Romeo and Juliet* talk? But there they were, giggling like they were in some kind of private comedy show.

And then it hits me.

Wait for it...

Jason and Taylor are perfect for each other.

And I actually felt something... good. Something that could almost be called relief. Not jealousy. Not even a little. I mean, why should I be jealous? It's not like I'm secretly in love with Jason or anything. Oh, wait, I might be.

Ugh.

So I do what any self-respecting human would do when faced with this bizarre, *complicated* emotional mess: I bury my face in my mashed potatoes. That's right. Because mashed potatoes are comforting, and I'm totally going to need a lot of comfort to figure out this whole "what do I even feel?" situation.

Later that day, as I'm sitting at my desk, trying to focus on the fact that Jason's tutoring session is *tomorrow* (tomorrow!), I catch myself doing something *really* embarrassing. I'm doodling. But it's not random doodles, no. It's Jake's name.

J-A-K-E.

With hearts.

Hearts. Seriously, Avery? Are you *seven*? I quickly try to erase it, but the eraser is doing this weird streaking thing, and now the whole page looks like it's been hit by an ink storm. I pull out a fresh sheet, but the damage is already done. The *heart-filled* disaster is forever etched into my brain.

That's it. I can't think straight. My feelings are a mess. I need to get my life together.

Time for a self-discovery quiz.

I go online and pull up a "Which Teen Romance Novel Character Are You?" quiz (because nothing says "self-discovery" like quizzes made by people who don't know me at all). As I answer questions like, "What would your perfect date be?" I realize the answers are way too specific, like "taking a hot air balloon ride with your soulmate," and I'm like, "Seriously? I'm just trying to figure out if I like Jake or Jason."

But I keep going, because what else is there to do? I answer questions about favorite colors, foods, and whether or not I'd choose to save my dog or my best friend from a bear. I'm *so* close to the end when Claire and Ellie sneak up behind me, and Claire immediately starts reading over my shoulder.

"Oh my gosh, Avery, are you... doodling Jake's name with hearts?" Claire says, her voice way too loud for someone who's supposed to be *subtly* sneaky.

I shake my head. "No, no, no! I wasn't... I mean, I wasn't doing that. What makes you think I—"

Ellie, who has somehow developed ninja-like reflexes, pops her head in and squints at my notebook. "Avery, that's like... a *full-on* heart attack right there. You're so obviously into him."

"No!" I yell, way too loudly. Everyone turns to look, and I can feel my face turning crimson. I mean, I've seen my face do this a lot, but this is the *deepest* shade of red I've ever experienced.

Claire raises her eyebrows. "Uh-huh. Okay, then why are you taking quizzes about 'perfect date ideas'?"

I just stare at the screen, my mind blank. The quiz results pop up, and according to it, I'm a "confident, independent adventurer." Which is funny, because the only "adventure" I'm dealing with right now is whether or not I'm going to accidentally spill juice on my shirt at lunch tomorrow. Definitely not the same thing.

"Don't look at me like that," I say, crossing my arms over my chest. "I was just curious, okay?"

Ellie giggles. "Sure, just curious. You're totally *obsessed* with Jake. We get it."

I throw my pencil at her. She ducks. "Stop it! I'm not obsessed!" I protest, but deep down, I know I sound like every movie character who says, "I'm not in love with him!" while doing the exact opposite.

At home that night, I'm trying to organize my notes for tomorrow's tutoring session with Jason (which I'm sure will go terribly because of all the weird thoughts swirling in my brain). But my attention is pulled away when Carl bursts into the room.

"Guess what I found?" he says, holding up a crumpled paper. "Avery's diary about Jake!"

"I don't have a diary!" I yell, snatching it from his hands. I scan the paper, and to my horror, it's a "Jake List" I apparently wrote TWO YEARS ago.

Jake's Best Features:

- The way his hair looks when he's doing math problems.
- The fact that he's so *smart* but doesn't brag about it.
- His laugh (it's like a kitten got tickled).

Carl snorts. "Looks like you like him." He walks out before I can even process what's just happened.

I fold the paper into a tiny square and stuff it in the back of my drawer. But now I'm definitely thinking about Jake's laugh. And maybe I *do* like him, and I'm just too stubborn to admit it.

I guess I'll just have to keep pretending like I *don't* like Jake. But the truth is, every time I think about him, it feels like I can't stop smiling. It's super annoying. And embarrassing. But also... kinda nice?

I've got a lot to figure out. But for now, I guess I'll just... distract myself with something else. Like self-discovery quizzes. Or maybe I should just eat more mashed potatoes.

8. The Bubble Bursts

Jason is still my main crush target, and I've decided today is the day he realizes how amazing I am. I try to walk past his locker casually, but I trip on someone's math book and faceplant right in front of him. Jason doesn't notice me sprawled on the ground, but he does pick up the math book and ask if this book is in Spanish.

"Spanish?!" Claire whispers later as we sit in the library. "Avery, I'm not saying Jason's not smart, but... okay, yes, I am saying that."

Ellie adds, "He also called a stapler a harmonica in English class last week."

I roll my eyes. "That was a joke. Jason's totally funny. He's just, like... ironic."

Claire and Ellie exchange a look, the kind that says *This girl is in deep denial.*

Still, their words stick in my head like gum on a shoe. And speaking of gum, Jason chews gum like a cow auditioning for a food commercial. I notice it for the first time in science when he pops a bubble so loud, it startles the teacher into spilling her coffee.

"Great job, Jason," the teacher says sarcastically, blotting her shirt with a paper towel.

Jason just grins. "Oops."

At lunch, Claire and Ellie sit with me, armed with "Jason proof."

"Exhibit A," Claire says, pointing at Jason across the cafeteria. "He's double-dipping his pizza crust into ketchup. WHO does that?"

"Maybe he likes his food... saucy?" I offer weakly.

"Exhibit B," Ellie continues, showing me a picture on her phone. It's from yesterday's math quiz, and Jason's paper has "X = ?" written across the top with no actual answer.

"He's creative!" I defend. "Math is about thinking outside the box!"

Claire raises an eyebrow. "Girl, he doesn't even know what box he's in."

The afternoon gets worse. Jason sits in front of me in history class, and as the teacher talks about the Civil War, Jason raises his hand and asks, "Wait, did they have cars back then?"

I feel my soul leave my body. Claire, sitting two rows over, pretends to play a tiny violin while Ellie tries not to burst out laughing.

Even Taylor, who's sitting next to Jason, politely says, "Um, no, Jason. No cars."

Jason shrugs. "Okay, just checking."

I catch myself staring at Jake, who's sitting by the window and sketching something in his notebook. Probably a masterpiece or a blueprint for saving the planet. Jake never asks if George Washington had a Ford Mustang.

By the time school ends, I'm questioning everything.

Claire and Ellie walk home with me, listing more "Jason flaws" while I try to cover my ears.

"He thought Pluto was still a planet," Claire says.
"He called a llama a 'weird giraffe' on the class trip," Ellie adds. "And don't forget the gum thing," Claire says.
"Oh, I noticed the gum thing," I mutter.

When I get home, I grab my diary and start writing furiously:
Reasons Jason Might Not Be Perfect

1. Chews gum like he's in a contest.
2. Thinks staplers are harmonicas.
3. Said the American Revolution was "a vibe."
4. Ketchup pizza crust—need I say more?

I slam the diary shut, but the truth is staring me in the face: Jason might not be my dream guy after all. And worse? I think I already know who is.

Dinner is chaos as usual. Grandpa decides it's a "slurp your soup" competition, and Carl pours soda into his mashed potatoes to "see what happens." Mom sighs and asks if I have any homework, but all I can think about is how Jason said Shakespeare "probably wrote for TikTok."

Jake's name pops into my brain again, and I groan, dropping my spoon into my soup.

"What's wrong with you?" Carl asks, licking a potato-covered spoon.

"Nothing!" I snap.

Grandpa winks. "Sounds like *love trouble.* Let me guess—does he chew gum too loud?"

I drop my head onto the table. "Why is this my life?"

After dinner, I head upstairs and open my diary again. This time, I make a new list:
Reasons Jake Might Be... Something

1. He doesn't chew gum like a maniac.
2. He knows Pluto is a dwarf planet.
3. He helped me untangle my scarf that one time and didn't laugh.
4. He's... nice.

I close the diary and stare at the ceiling. What if Jake *is* nice? What if nice is better than "vibes" and ketchup pizza?

Suddenly, my phone buzzes with a text. It's from Jake:
Found your water bottle in the library. Want me to bring it tomorrow?

I smile at the screen and text back:
Thanks. And yes. And maybe... bring snacks too?

The Jason bubble officially bursts the next day when he says Romeo and Juliet should've "just texted each other instead of dying." Even Taylor rolls her eyes at that one.

As for me? I'm starting to realize that maybe I've been looking in the wrong direction all along.

9. Ice Packs and Awkward Chats

Gym class is basically where dignity goes to die. Today's activity: dodgeball, aka "Let's See How Fast We Can Humiliate Avery." Our gym teacher, Mr. Graham, splits us into teams and gives his usual pep talk about how dodgeball builds "teamwork and resilience," which is gym-teacher code for "Prepare to get kicked in the face."

I pick a spot in the back corner, hoping to stay out of the action. My strategy is simple: be invisible. Unfortunately, some random girl on the other team has the throwing arm of a pro pitcher and the aim of a hawk.

"Avery, watch out!" Claire yells.

Too late.

The ball smacks me square in the nose, and I drop to the floor like a deflated balloon. Everything feels blurry and wobbly, and for a second, I'm pretty sure I've lost my sense of smell forever.

When I finally sit up, Jake is standing over me, holding an ice pack.

"Impressive defense skills," he says, grinning. "You really showed that ball who's boss."

"Ha. Ha," I mutter, holding the ice pack to my face. My nose feels like it's been flattened into a pancake.

Mr. Graham jogs over, looking mildly concerned but mostly annoyed. "Avery, you okay? You know this is dodgeball, not drama class, right?"

I glare at him. "Pretty sure I'm not acting."

Jake snorts, and Mr. Graham tells me to "shake it off" before jogging back to his whistle-blowing duties.

"Classic Graham," Jake says. "The man's got the emotional range of a potato."

That makes me laugh, which hurts my nose but is totally worth it.

Jake sits next to me on the bleachers while I ice my face. "So, how does it feel to be the MVP of dodgeball?"

"I'm pretty sure MVP stands for 'Most Victimized Player,'" I reply.

Jake grins. "Well, if it makes you feel better, you've got a killer bruise forming. Very intimidating."

"Great," I say. "I'll scare off all the dodgeballs now."

We sit there for a few minutes, watching the chaos unfold on the court. Someone screams, someone else trips, and I spot Claire hiding behind Ellie like a human shield.

"So," Jake says, breaking the silence. "Read anything good lately?"

The question catches me off guard. Jake and I used to talk about books all the time when we were little kids, but that feels like forever ago.

"Uh, not really," I say. "Unless you count my science textbook, which, spoiler alert, I don't."

Jake laughs. "You should read *The Midnight Code.* It's about this group of kids who solve a mystery using these cryptic riddles. Totally up your alley."

"Sounds cool," I say, trying not to sound too eager. "I'll check it out."

"Cool," Jake says. He leans back on the bleachers, looking totally relaxed, while I sit there trying not to overanalyze the fact that we're having an actual conversation.

Later, in the locker room, Claire and Ellie corner me.

"What was that?" Claire demands, waving her hands around like a detective interrogating a suspect.

"What was what?" I ask, pretending to be clueless.

"You and Jake!" Ellie says. "You were all... talking and laughing and—wait, are you blushing?"

"No!" I say, definitely blushing.

Claire squints at me. "You totally are. Oh my gosh, do you like him?"

"Can we not do this right now?" I groan, shoving my stuff into my gym bag.

Ellie gasps. "You DO like him!"

By the time I get home, my head is spinning. Between dodgeball disasters, Jake being all nice and funny, and Claire and Ellie turning into amateur matchmakers, I'm ready to collapse.

At dinner, Grandpa notices my nose and says, "Looks like you went a few rounds with a grizzly bear."

Carl, of course, thinks this is hilarious. "Did you lose?"

Mom sighs. "Carl, stop teasing your sister. Avery, do you need more ice?"

"I'm fine," I say, stabbing my food a little harder than necessary.

Carl smirks at me across the table. "So, when's the wedding?"

I drop my fork. "He's NOT my boyfriend!"

Carl starts chanting, "Avery's got a boyfriend!" until Mom sends him to his room."

After dinner, I flop onto my bed and grab my diary.
Dear Diary,
Today, I got smacked in the face with a dodgeball and had an actual conversation with Jake. He recommended a book, which is normal, right? Friends recommend books to each other. Friends also don't make your heart do weird flippy things, so maybe I need to stop overthinking this.

I stare at the page for a minute before adding:
P.S. Dodgeball is the worst sport ever invented.

10. Jake and the Flying Snack Attack

It's Saturday, which is supposed to be my day of peace. A day of rest. A day where I lounge around in my pajamas and eat an entire bag of chips without anyone judging me. Instead, I'm sprinting through the house, yelling, "CARL, I'M GOING TO END YOU!"

Why? Because Carl, my *dear* little brother, has decided to make my life a living nightmare.

Here's what happens: I'm on the phone with Claire, talking about random stuff, when somehow the topic drifts to Jake. I don't even realize it, but I must've said something like, "He's pretty cool," in a way that's less *chill casual* and more *crushing hard*. The next thing I know, Carl, who must have supersonic hearing, pops out of nowhere like he's been summoned and starts singing at the top of his lungs:

"Avery and Jake, sittin' in a tree! K-I-S-" "CARL!" I shout, my face burning hotter than Mom's mystery meatloaf.

"He's already gone, sprinting through the living room like some kind of annoying gremlin. "First comes love, then comes marriage!" he shouts, dodging furniture like he's training for the Olympics. I chase after him, yelling, "GET BACK HERE!" but Carl's got the speed of a squirrel fueled by sugar and chaos. I'm running full speed when Whiskers, our cranky old cat, decides this is the perfect time to nap in the middle of the hallway.

"NOOOOOOOOOOOOOOO!" I yell, but it's too late. My foot catches on Whiskers, and the next thing I know Me *and* Whiskers are flying through the air like two clueless rockets on a crash course. I flail my arms like I'm trying to high-five the ceiling, and Whiskers looks up like, "Really? *Now* you decide to trip on me?"

And then it happens.

The popcorn bowl. The giant, family-sized bowl of popcorn I made just ten minutes ago to enjoy my *peaceful Saturday*. It launches into the air like a confetti cannon at a birthday party.

I crash to the ground with a loud "Oof!" Popcorn rains down everywhere—on the couch, on the rug, on *me*. But the worst part?

Jake. Standing at the front door. Holding a book. And now also holding a FACE FULL OF POPCORN.

"Uhhh..." I say, frozen on the floor like a total idiot. My brain is screaming, *Why is he here?! Why is he HERE?!*

Jake brushes some popcorn off his shirt, looks at the mess, and—laughs. Like, really laughs. Not just a polite chuckle, but the kind of laugh where you're shaking and can't breathe.

"That," he says, still laughing, "was the most epic thing I've ever seen."

I blink. "You're not mad?"

"Mad?" Jake grins. "Are you kidding? That was amazing. You could've gone pro with a popcorn toss like that."

Carl, who has been hiding behind the couch watching this disaster unfold, pops up and shouts, "See? I TOLD you Avery and Jake were a thing!"

"CARL!" I screech, throwing a handful of popcorn at him.

Jake just laughs harder. "So, uh," he says, holding up the book, "I thought you might want this. It's the book we talked about yesterday."

My heart does this weird little flip-flop thing, but I tell it to calm down. It's just a book. Just a thoughtful, sweet, perfect book. No big deal.

"Thanks," I mumble, trying to sound casual as I take it from him.

"No problem," Jake says, still smiling. "I'll let you get back to..." He glances at the popcorn-covered living room. "Whatever this is."

He heads out, leaving me standing there like a human tomato, clutching the book like it's a trophy.

Carl leans over and smirks. "Sooooo... Jake's your boyfriend now?"

I grab a couch cushion and chase him through the house all over again.

11. Explosions, Messes, and Maybe Feelings

It's the day of the science project, and I'm feeling a mixture of nervousness and dread. The kind of feeling you get when you realize you're about to create a chemical disaster with baking soda. The project is supposed to be "simple," but simple in science class means you're going to end up with a disaster that looks like a volcano erupted in your kitchen. And guess what? That's exactly what happens.

I meet Jake at our assigned lab table, which is, surprise surprise, covered in a ridiculous amount of baking soda. Jake's already wearing safety goggles, but instead of looking smart, he looks like a confused guinea pig. He waves at me like we're in a sitcom.

"Ready to make history?" he asks, tapping a plastic bottle with a spoon.

I nod, trying not to be completely distracted by the fact that Jake looks even cooler today. Maybe it's his height—he's suddenly much taller than me, like a skyscraper. Maybe it's the way he keeps pushing his hair out of his eyes. Or maybe it's the way he smiles when he says things like, "You know, we could totally make this volcano explode if we add *just* the right amount of baking soda and vinegar."

But here's the thing: I'm not sure how much *right* is involved when you're working with substances that can create explosions. But hey, no one's told me that yet, so I just smile back like I know what I'm doing. Spoiler alert: I absolutely do not know what I'm doing.

"Okay, so we just pour in the vinegar now, right?" Jake asks, holding the bottle with a look of pure, unfiltered excitement.

"Sure," I say, even though I don't know what we're supposed to be doing. I grab the vinegar, ready to cause an explosion of our own. When I pour it in, *nothing* happens. I pour more. Still nothing.

"Maybe we need more baking soda?" I suggest, trying to sound like I know anything about science.

"More baking soda?" Jake asks, his voice rising with a mix of disbelief and hope. "Are you sure we're not going to flood the whole classroom?"

"Flood the classroom?" I ask, now more concerned about the disaster I'm about to create than my science grade. But then, of course, things get worse. I shake the bottle of vinegar with desperation, as if I could force the explosion to happen with sheer willpower. And that's when the whole thing blows up—*everywhere.*

The vinegar shoots up, splashing everywhere like it's on a mission. And of course, it's not just any vinegar—it smells like it's been sitting in a moldy sock for a year. It lands in my hair, down my shirt, and—yep—right on my face. I scream and rub my eyes, but then I hear Jake laughing."

Not just any laugh. It's the kind of laugh that makes you want to laugh too, even though your face smells like an expired pickle. It's the good, infectious kind that makes everything feel a little less horrible.

"Oh my gosh, you look like a science experiment gone wrong," Jake says, still grinning.

I blink, realizing that I probably look like a cross between a swamp monster and someone who's just been rejected by a toothpaste commercial. "Great. Just great," I mutter.

Jake offers me a paper towel. "You might want to clean up, but at least the volcano is doing its job."

I look at the tiny eruption that's now spreading over the table like a sticky mess. "That... wasn't supposed to happen."

"Nope," Jake agrees, leaning back in his chair, watching the mess spread like it's the next big thing in science. "But it's impressive. Definitely 'A+' material, right?"

I laugh, but then something weird happens. It's like a switch flips in my brain. I stop worrying about the disaster and start focusing on how Jake's smile is brighter than the volcano explosion. I mean, he's laughing at our failure, and somehow, that makes me feel better about the whole thing.

And then, as if things weren't confusing enough, Jake asks, "So, do you ever miss when we used to hang out all the time?"

And it's like the world stops for a second. I stare at him, my brain trying to catch up with what he just said. He used the word *miss*. As in, we used to be friends before everything got weird. Before I started having all these *feelings* that make me want to do cartwheels and not talk about them.

I gulp. "Uh, maybe?" I stammer, my heart doing this awkward tap dance in my chest. I try to sound casual, but it's impossible when your feelings are suddenly more jumbled than your science project. I quickly change the subject. "Hey, uh, we should clean this up before Mrs. Johnson comes over and yells at us for making a mess."

Jake raises an eyebrow. "You sure? Because it looks like a real masterpiece to me."

I groan, feeling a wave of *ugh* wash over me. "Yeah, because nothing says 'masterpiece' like a sticky puddle of vinegar on the floor."

But even as I say that, I'm secretly wishing we could just stand here for a little longer. It feels comfortable. Jake feels comfortable.

Just as the silence gets awkward, Jake says, "Still can't believe you thought vinegar and soda wouldn't erupt."

I groan. "Thanks for pointing that out, genius."

Jake smirks. "Next time, maybe read the directions? Or avoid vinegar that smells like it's been in the back of the fridge for a year."

I laugh, tossing a soggy paper towel at him. "Noted. You're in charge next time."

"Deal," he says, wiping up the mess. Then, out of nowhere, he adds, "You're pretty good at this stuff. You've always been... creative."

Creative? Me? I wasn't expecting that. "Uh, thanks?" I say, feeling weird but kind of happy.

Jake shrugs. "Don't let it go to your head."

I laugh again, but inside, I'm totally freaking out. What is happening here?

As we finish cleaning up, I can't help but think about how easy it feels to hang out with Jake, even when things go totally wrong. I didn't realize how much I missed this—laughing, joking, and just being around him—it feels like having my old best friend back.

12. Best Week Ever... Sort Of

Here's how it starts: I'm at my locker, minding my own business, trying to stuff a very rebellious math textbook into my backpack. Suddenly, out of nowhere, Jake is just THERE, leaning against the lockers like some kind of cool movie character.

"Hey, Avery," he says, like it's no big deal.

Meanwhile, my brain? NOT. FUNCTIONING. I freeze mid-textbook shove, which is bad timing because the stupid thing slides right back out of my bag and lands on my foot.

"OW!" I yell, hopping on one foot like an injured flamingo.

"You okay?" Jake asks, his voice full of concern but also a little bit of a laugh because, apparently, my pain is hilarious.

"Totally fine!" I squeak, even though my foot is throbbing and my dignity is somewhere down the hall.

Jake bends down, picks up the evil textbook, and hands it to me. "These things are dangerous. They should come with a warning label."

I laugh way too hard at that joke. Like, embarrassing-snort-laugh hard. And then I cover my face with my hands because, GREAT, now I'm officially the Weird Snort Girl.

But Jake just smiles. "So, I was thinking..."

Oh no. Thinking? That sounds serious. I brace myself for whatever's coming, clutching my textbook like it's a shield.

"I've kind of always liked you," he says, all casual, like he's telling me the weather or something.

WAIT. WHAT?!

I blink at him, my brain trying to catch up. "You... what?"

Jake scratches the back of his neck, looking a little nervous now. "You know, back when we used to play video games after school and stuff. I just... I thought you should know."

I'm pretty sure my face is on fire. Like, full tomato mode. My mouth opens, but no sound comes out because apparently, I've forgotten how to human.

Jake tilts his head, his smile turning into a grin. "It's okay if you don't feel the same way. I just thought I'd—"

"I LIKE YOU TOO!" I blurt out, way louder than I intended. My voice echoes down the hall, and I immediately slap a hand over my mouth.

Jake's grin turns into the biggest, happiest smile I've ever seen. "Really?"

"Yeah," I mumble through my fingers, still bright red. "You're, uh... cool. And nice. And, um... tall?" UGH. WHY DID I SAY THAT?

"Tall, huh?" Jake teases, laughing. "Well, thanks, I guess."

Before I can dig myself into a deeper hole, he asks, "So, do you maybe want to go skating with me sometime? Like, the rink by the park?"

My brain is SCREAMING, and I'm pretty sure my heart just did a backflip. "I'd love that," I say, trying to sound normal but probably failing because I'm grinning like a crazy person.

"Cool," Jake says, like this is just a normal conversation and not the BIGGEST MOMENT OF MY LIFE. "I'll text you later."

And then he waves and walks away, leaving me standing there like a statue, clutching my textbook and replaying the entire thing in my head on a loop.

The second he's out of sight, I bolt to the library. Not because I need to study, but because I need to HIDE and process what just happened.

In the library, I grab a random book off the shelf and sit down at a table, pretending to read while my brain keeps replaying Jake's words. "I've kind of always liked you." Like, WHAT?! When? How? WHY?

My phone buzzes, and it's a text from Claire: *"DID YOU SAY YES?!"*

I groan. Of course, she already knows. Probably Ellie, too. These two are like detectives when it comes to my life.

I type back, *"Yes. But don't make it a thing, okay?"*

Claire responds immediately: *"TOO LATE! THIS IS A HUGE THING!!!"*

I groan again, sinking lower into my chair. Whiskers, my cat, has more chill than my friends right now.

Later that night, I write everything down in my diary because, honestly, I need to get it out of my head before it explodes.

"It's official: this week has been the weirdest, most chaotic, and BEST week of my life. Also, I need skating lessons."

I close the diary, feeling a mix of excitement and nerves. I don't know what's going to happen next, but for the first time in a long time, I feel like maybe things are going to be okay.

Maybe even better than okay.

Printed in Great Britain
by Amazon